MAKING HISTORY

EGYPT in the time of RAMESES II

Written by
Jacqueline Morley

Illustrated by
Nicholas Hewetson

SIMON & SCHUSTER
YOUNG BOOKS

Contents

INTRODUCTION	3
AT HOME	4
A NOBLEMAN'S VILLA	6
THE RIVER NILE	8
THE PHARAOH	10
AT SCHOOL	12
THE ARMY	14
BUILDING A TEMPLE	16
THE GODS	18
GODS AND TEMPLES	20
PREPARING A MUMMY	22
THE FUNERAL	24
AN EGYPTIAN FARM	26
HUNTING	28
ENTERTAINING FRIENDS	30
IMPORTANT DATES	32
INDEX	32

DESIGN	DAVID SALARIYA
EDITOR	PENNY CLARKE
CONSULTANT	ROSALIE DAVID

FIRST PUBLISHED IN ITALY BY
GIUNTI GRUPPO EDITORIALE, FIRENZE
UNDER THE TITLE NELL' EGITTO DI RAMESSE II

THIS EDITION FIRST PUBLISHED IN 1993 BY
SIMON & SCHUSTER YOUNG BOOKS
CAMPUS 400
MAYLANDS AVENUE
HEMEL HEMPSTEAD
HERTS HP2 7EZ

© 1989 BY GIUNTI GRUPPO EDITORIALE
ENGLISH VERSION © 1993 BY
SIMON & SCHUSTER YOUNG BOOKS

ISBN 0 7500 1341 9 (HARDBACK)
ISBN 0 7500 1342 7 (PAPERBACK)

ALL RIGHTS RESERVED.

A CATALOGUE RECORD FOR THIS BOOK IS AVAILABLE FROM THE BRITISH LIBRARY.

PRINTED IN ITALY BY GIUNTI Industrie Grafiche

Introduction

THE CIVILIZATION OF ANCIENT EGYPT is one of the world's oldest and it lasted over three thousand years. Any civilization that lasts a long time will have its ups and downs, and Ancient Egypt was no exception. Eventually, after several weak rulers, it became part of the Roman Empire in 30 BC.

Scholars divide the history of Ancient Egypt into several periods. The Old Kingdom, the Middle Kingdom and the New Kingdom are the most important. During this time Egypt's rulers were known as 'pharaohs', a word meaning 'Great House'. This book is about life in Egypt during the reign of the pharaoh Rameses II, who ruled during the New Kingdom from about 1290 to about 1223 BC.

The New Kingdom was the time of Egypt's greatest wealth and power. Rameses II ruled a vast empire stretching from the Mediterranean Sea in the north to Nubia (roughly modern Sudan) in the south. Egypt had always been prosperous, thanks to the River Nile, but now all the conquered lands paid taxes to the pharaoh and the country became richer than ever. Rameses II used some of this wealth to build temples and palaces. The great temple of Abu Simbel (pages 16 and 17) was built on his orders and to his glory.

During the long span of Ancient Egypt's history, rulers came and went, battles were won and lost, but the lives of the ordinary people altered very little. Their lives were closely linked to the annual flooding of the Nile and that didn't change.

Religion and a belief in life after death were very important to the Egyptians. They believed the next life would be just like life on earth, so in their tombs they put the tools, clothes, furniture and other things they'd known so that they could use them in the next life. On the tomb walls they painted scenes of the life they'd left. This makes it possible for us to know a lot about the Ancient Egyptians although they lived so long ago.

At Home

▷ All wealthy Egyptians have many servants. There are servants to cook, to clean the house, to look after the family's clothes and the wigs that all rich Egyptians wear. This servant will sweep the roof then lay out figs and grapes to dry in the sun.

T**HE HOUSE SHOWN HERE** belongs to a wealthy Egyptian, an official at the court of the pharaoh Rameses II. It is set in a large courtyard with a pool and palm trees. As well as giving fruit, the vines are trained to make a shady area for the family to sit in.

All the work in the garden, and also in the house, is done by servants who live in small buildings in a separate courtyard at the back of their master's house.

Servants carried their masters through the busy streets in special chairs.

This house is much larger than most Egyptian homes, but it is similar to them in many ways. It is built of mud bricks dried in the sun's heat, and it has a flat roof. The windows are small and set high up in the walls, because this helps to keep the heat out. The roof projects to form a wide porch, which also helps to keep the rooms cool. The columns supporting the porch have been decorated. At the top they are shaped like the bud of the lotus, a sacred water plant that grows in the River Nile. The outside walls are painted with a kind of whitewash to reflect the heat of the sun.

Even today, many Egyptian homes use the same means to keep cool: flat roofs, small windows and porches.

◁ This pool is not just decorative, though the family's children will probably swim in it. The gardeners use it to water their master's garden through the long, hot summer.

A Nobleman's Villa

THE ILLUSTRATIONS ON THESE two pages are based on excavations archaeologists have made at Tel-el-Amarna. This city was built by the pharaoh Akhenaten who reigned from 1656 to 1625 BC, about 60 years before Rameses II.

1 Vase for kohl, a black eye make-up.
2 Tongs to curl wigs.
3 Polished bronze mirror.
4 Bronze razor for shaving the head.
5 Comb.
6 Force-feeding a duck to fatten it.
7 Cooking a goose.

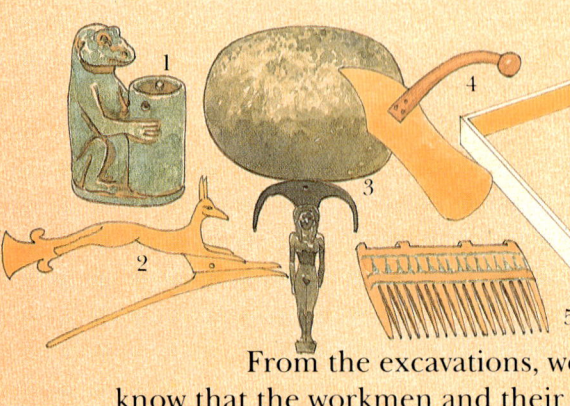

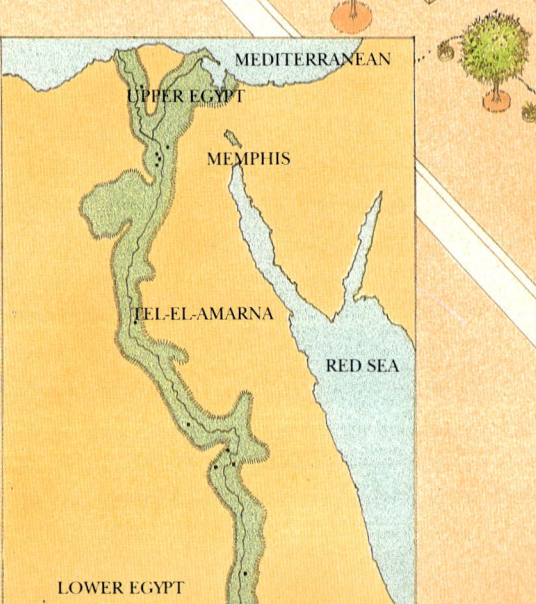

From the excavations, we know that the workmen and their families lived in small four-roomed houses packed closely together along narrow streets, so a villa as grand as this must have belonged to a very important nobleman. Much of the villa has been drawn without its roof, to show the size and layout of the rooms.

The furniture was very simple, even in homes as grand as this. The short-legged tables, chairs and low stools were moved from room to room as people needed them. There were no cupboards; instead the Egyptians used chests, boxes and baskets for storage. Most furniture was wooden, though some was made from the thick strong reeds that grew by the Nile. Lamps burning oil lit the rooms at night.

8 Chest for storing clothes.
9 Stool.
10 Bed.
11 Head-rest.
12 Chair.
13–15 Children's toys.

A Private chapel
B Well
C Entrance
D Main room
E The master's room
F Granaries
G Stables
H Women's quarters
I Servants' rooms
J Toilets and wash-rooms

16 Sandal of plaited papyrus. Sandals like this were also made of leather and sometimes even of gold.
17 Gold earrings like these were popular among the wealthy.
18 Gold bracelets, another example of the skill of Egyptian craftsmen.

Egyptian craftsmen were very skilled and archaeologists have found chests made from rare woods, beautifully inlaid with ivory and semi-precious stones. The owner of this villa and his family probably used such chests.

7

The River Nile

THE RIVER NILE WAS source of Ancient Egypt's wealth. Each year the river overflowed its banks, covering the land with mud and silt. This made the land fertile, with good crops. Without the annual flood the land beside the Nile would be a desert like the rest of the country.

The Nile was also Egypt's highway. There were no proper roads in the desert or in the marshy delta where the Nile flows into the Mediterranean Sea. Everything in Egypt went by river, and even the smallest village on the river's banks had a jetty where farmers could load and unload their crops. Larger places, like Tel-el-Amarna, had busy port areas.

Many of the boats on the Nile came from distant countries. Timber from Syria in the north arrived in big sea-going ships. From Nubia, to the south, boats brought copper, ivory, ostrich and animal skins.

This trade brought more wealth to the pharaohs because many of goods were taxed. Customs officials checked the cargoes to find out how much tax had to be paid on each load.

◁ The Ancient Egyptians did not use money, so all the goods set out on this quayside would be exchanged for other goods in a form of barter. Everything was valued in units known as 'debens' and it was up to the buyer and the seller to agree the goods they would exchange when making a 'sale'.

We know from records found in a tomb that an ox valued at 130 debens was 'sold' for a linen tunic worth 60 debens, fruit worth 20 debens, beads for a necklace worth 30 debens and two cheap tunics worth only 10 debens each. It may sound very complicated, but imagine explaining our money system!

The Pharaoh

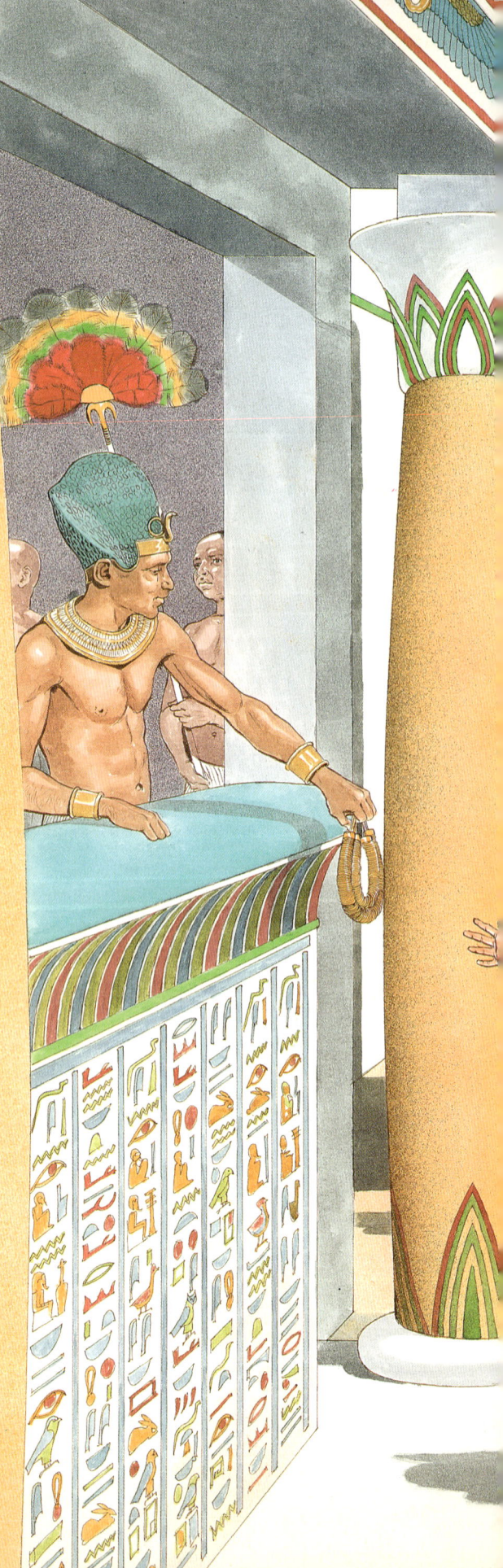

To THE EGYPTIANS THEIR pharaoh was a god. They believed he was Horus, the falcon god, reborn as a man, and also the son of Re, the sun god. Because he was a god he was all-powerful. The land and everything that lived on it belonged to the pharaoh. He was the chief judge, the high priest and the commander of the army. He made the laws and decided the country's foreign policy, which, under Rameses II, meant many wars and conquests.

Of course the pharaoh couldn't do everything. A large civil service of officials organized the day-to-day government of the country. They worked under the chief minister, the vizier. He was appointed, and dismissed if necessary, by the pharaoh.

If the pharaoh was pleased with one of his officials – perhaps an architect who had designed a fine building – he rewarded him at a special ceremony. One of the palace courtyards had a balcony magnificently decorated with gold and semi-precious stones. The pharaoh would appear on the balcony and in front of cheering crowds present his official with a gold collar or some other valuable gift. All Egyptian officials hoped that they would receive such an honour because the gift came from a god, not a man. Or so the Egyptian people believed.

◁ We know from tomb-paintings and archaeological excavations that the palaces of the pharaohs were elaborately decorated. (Egypt's dry climate is the reason why so many remains from so long ago survive.)

Rameses II had a large number of statues made of himself, many times life-size. They were intended to show just how powerful and important – and god-like – he was. These statues often show him wearing a crown with a cobra on the front. The Egyptians believed that cobras were particularly sacred and powerful protection against enemies.

△ Wherever the pharaoh went he was accompanied by royal fan-bearers, rather like flags are used on special occasions today. These fans were often made from coloured ostrich feathers, imported into Egypt along the Nile from countries far to the south. However, evidence, again from tomb-paintings, also suggests that there were ostriches in Ancient Egypt.

11

At School

VERY FEW PEOPLE IN Rameses II's kingdom could read or write. Only the children of nobles or high officials had any education. Girls from these families were taught at home, while their brothers went off to the school run by the priests at a nearby temple. Discipline at these schools was strict, and lazy or careless boys were beaten.

In any society where few people can read or write, those people who can have a great advantage over the others. It was like this in Ancient Egypt. Learning to read and write was the first step towards a good career. Boys who did well at school could become scribes, or professional writers. All the departments of the government kept careful written records of business and legal matters. Archaeologists have found notes about trade, taxes and foreign affairs, as well as lists of military supplies and equipment. So there was plenty of employment for any boy who could read and write well. There were opportunities for promotion, too. The vizier, the pharaoh's chief official, had started his career as a scribe.

Children from ordinary families learnt a trade or craft as soon as they were old enough, usually their father's. Country children learnt about farming by helping their parents.

12

▽ At school the boys wrote on pieces of broken pottery or large flakes of limestone. Although the Egyptians invented paper, making it from the papyrus plant that grows beside the Nile, it was far too expensive and precious for schoolboys to use.

Written work was done with a reed pen in black or red ink.

Pieces of pottery with exercises written on them have survived. One boy wrote beside his work: Lesson time lasts for ever!

▽ The Egyptian summers were too hot to wear many clothes. The teacher wears a sort of kilt made of linen, while the boys just wear loincloths. The boys all wear sandals like those on page 7.

In the temple the priest will have his head bare and shaved, but in school he wears a woollen wig. Each boy has a plait.

13

▽ Shooting arrows from a chariot pulled by galloping horses across rough ground was very difficult. The chariots were light, for extra speed, so jolted and skidded at every bump in the ground, making an accurate aim extremely hard.

▽ The pharaoh's body armour was of leather covered with gold discs rather like scales.

The Army

RAMESES II WAS A great warrior. He was ten years old when he first led a band of soldiers into battle.

When he became pharaoh he continued this war-like approach, attacking the kingdoms on the borders of Egypt. He was a fearless fighter and once, at the battle of Kadesh, he defeated the enemy almost single-handed because most of the Egyptian army had fled. His pet lion always accompanied him into battle, terrifying the enemy's soldiers.

The Egyptian army was divided into four regiments, each named after a god: Amun, Re, Phtah and Seth. Each regiment was made up of infantry (foot soldiers), archers and chariot troops. The chariot troops all came from rich or noble families, because only they could afford a chariot and pair of swift horses.

Horses were unknown in Egypt until around 1600 BC, when the country was invaded by the Hyksos. The Hyksos were a nomadic people from the north who first entered Egypt by the mouth of the Nile. They fought from horse-drawn chariots, easily overwhelming the Egyptian forces who were all on foot. In time, the Egyptians learnt their lesson, copied the Hyksos and eventually defeated them.

In battle, the chariot troops would charge through the ranks of the enemy to break them up and cause confusion. Having done that, the chariots were wheeled round and the enemy attacked from the rear.

After the battle was over, the right hands of the dead enemy soldiers were cut off and put in piles. In this way the Egyptians could find out how many had been killed.

△ The temple at Abu Simbel was carved from the sandstone rock. It is quite a soft rock, but the Egyptians only had hand tools to work with, mostly made of stone or bronze. Bronze is quite a soft metal and so wears out easily.

Hieroglyphs, the symbols the Egyptians used to express themselves, cover every inch of the temple's front that is not a statue.

Scribes kept detailed records of the temple's progress and the workmen's excuses for absence!

▷ The royal boat has brought Rameses II to inspect the progress of his new temple. Everything that is needed on the site has to be brought there by boat.

Building a Temple

To mark the thirtieth anniversary of his reign, Rameses II decided to build a temple at Abu Simbel dedicated to Re, the sun god, and to Rameses himself. The Egyptians believed that keeping the gods happy was very important and that building temples was the best way of doing this.

Carving the temple out of a hillside overlooking the Nile was an enormous project, needing hundreds of workmen. First the side of the hill had to be chipped away to make the south front of the temple. The draughtsmen marked out the doorways and the four huge statues of Rameses that would form the front of the temple. Stone masons cut out the rough shapes of the statues, then skilled carvers sculpted the heads and bodies, smoothing them with polishing stones. Others carved the hieroglyphs recounting Rameses II's victories.

While all this was going on, the interior of the temple was hollowed out of the hill. This was done by slaves, mostly prisoners-of-war. The finished temple had three rooms, each containing still more statues carved out of the rock and covered with scenes of Rameses's many victories.

The Gods

THE EGYPTIANS WORSHIPPED MANY gods and goddesses. Most of them represented natural forces which the Egyptians didn't understand. At that time, over 3,000 years ago, no-one knew the cause of thunder or lightning, earthquakes or even why the Nile flooded each year. Instead, people thought they were controlled by powerful gods.

Each town and village had its own special god (or goddess), such as the Apis-bull of Memphis. Other gods, such as Re the sun god and Nut the sky goddess, were believed to be so powerful that everyone worshipped them.

In statues and paintings, the Egyptians' gods are often shown as animals or birds. For example, Apis was a bull, Bubastis a cat, Anubis had the head of a jackal and Horus the head of a falcon. All these creatures were common in Egypt at this time.

Each god and goddess had a special festival day. There were processions and feasting and dancing as the statue of the god was taken through the streets to the temple. The statue was kept covered so that ordinary people could not see it, because they were believed to be unworthy to look at a god. They were not allowed into the temple either, but they could leave their offerings to the god in the courtyard of the temple. Offerings of food were part of the priests' wages.

▽ Crowds line the streets to watch the procession as the god's statue passes by. On a god's special festival day, everyone has a holiday.

▷ Shaven-headed priests carry the golden shrine containing the statue of Amun, the wind god, down to the Nile. The procession is led by priests carrying ceremonial feather fans. Musicians and singers accompany the procession.

The shrine is covered in gold, because gold had great religious importance for the Ancient Egyptians. They did not think it valuable, like we do. Instead, they believed that gold was the flesh of Re, the sun god, and so was sacred.

Gods and Temples

◁ The scarab (or sacred beetle) was a symbol of Re, the sun god. It is often shown, as here, pushing the sun's disc in front of it. The Egyptians believed scarabs had magic powers.

By RAMESES II'S REIGN, all temples were built to the same design. The sanctuary, where the statue of the god (or goddess) stood, was the most important part. To reach the sanctuary, the priests had to go through many different courtyards and halls, decorated with imaginary scenes from the life of the god. Near each temple were schools, libraries and store-rooms, and also homes for all those who looked after the temple: priests, craftsmen and ordinary workmen.

The Egyptians believed that Nut, the sky goddess, arched her body over the earth, with her feet in the east and her hands in the west. Her father Shu, god of the air, held her up above her brother Geb, god of the earth.

△ Section through a temple built in the time of Rameses II.
A Entrance
B Courtyard
C Hall with columns
D Sanctuary.

The walls of rooms in a temple like this would have been decorated with paintings of the many gods the Ancient Egyptians worshipped. Among the chief gods were:
1 Atun, creator and ruler of the world
2 Isis, Osiris' wife, protector of children.
3 Osiris, god of the underworld and judge of the dead.
4 Horus, god of the day, son of Isis and Osiris.
5 Anubis, the jackal-headed god of the dead.

20

The Egyptians explained the sequence of day and night by their idea that Re, the sun god, travelled across the sky each day in a boat – just as the Egyptians travelled on the Nile. Each evening Re's mother, Nut, swallowed him, then gave birth to him again in the morning.

The Ancient Egyptians did not have an alphabet like ours. Instead, to write, they used small pictorial symbols known as hieroglyphs. Scribes in Rameses II's time had to know about 700 different hieroglyphs.

6 Hathor was the goddess of pleasure, dancing and love.
7 Re, the sun god, was the supreme god during Rameses II's reign.

Preparing a Mummy

THE EGYPTIANS BELIEVED THAT there was a life after death. According to them, when someone died the soul went on living and needed its body to return to. So the body was carefully preserved in a process called mummification.

The dead person's body was taken to the embalmers, skilled men who treated it so that it would not decay. First they took out the brains and internal organs like the heart, placing them in special jars. Then the body was washed and cleaned, filled with sweet-smelling spices and covered with natron, a kind of soda. After 70 days the body would be quite dry and preserved. Then it was cleaned again and rubbed with special oils. If the dead person had been rich, the body was also decorated with fine jewellery.

Next the mummy was carefully wrapped in long linen bandages. Magic objects called amulets were put between the layers of bandage to give extra protection in the next life.

Finally, the mummy was put in a coffin shaped like a human figure. These coffins were often richly decorated with paintings of the gods and accounts of the dead person's life. Only then was a person ready for the journey across the Nile and the start of the next life.

▽ The embalmers had to work quickly: a dead body soon starts to decay in a hot climate. They removed the brain, the heart and other organs and put them in special jars, called canopic jars. Each jar, which was usually made of pottery, had a top modelled in the shape of a human, a baboon, a dog or a falcon. The jars were put in a special box and buried with the mummy.

▷ The body's organs were removed through an opening cut just below the ribs. After everything was taken out and the body packed with spices and herbs, the opening was sewn up again to keep the body in its proper shape. It was then ready to be wrapped in linen bandages.

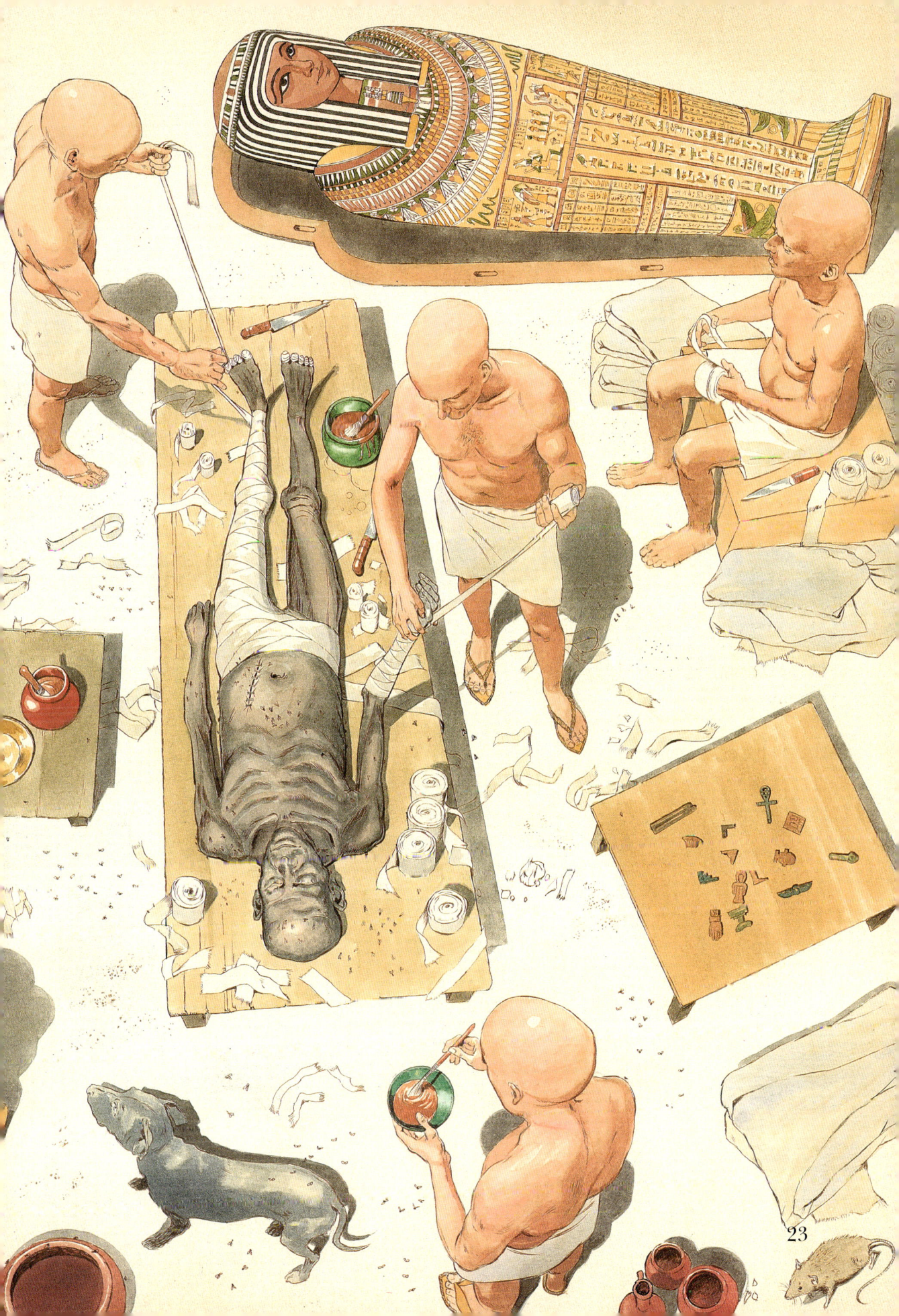

The Funeral

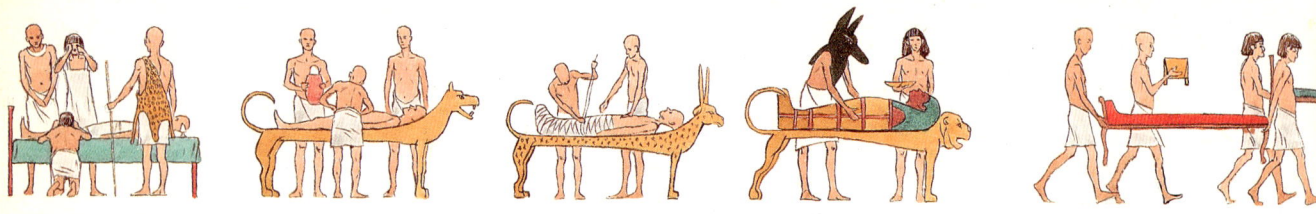

Scenes showing an Egyptian funeral. Archaeologists have found many tombs decorated with scenes like these. First, the family mourns the dead person, then the body is taken to the embalmers for mummification. The funeral procession forms, and servants bring the furniture and other goods for the next life.

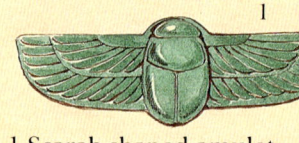

E GYPTIAN CEMETERIES WERE ON the Nile's west bank, because the sun set, or died, in the west. Most people lived on the east bank, so funerals meant crossing the river. This symbolized the journey of Re's boat across the sky and the journey to the dead person's new life.

Priests put the coffin on a bier covered with a canopy. The bier was on a sledge pulled by oxen and headed the funeral procession to the Nile. Professional mourners tore their clothes and threw dust on their heads as signs of grief. Servants followed with furniture and clothes for use in the next world.

1 Scarab-shaped amulet.
2 Canopic jars, and the box to hold them.
3 Amulets from a mummy.
4 Model of a funeral boat with the coffin on board.

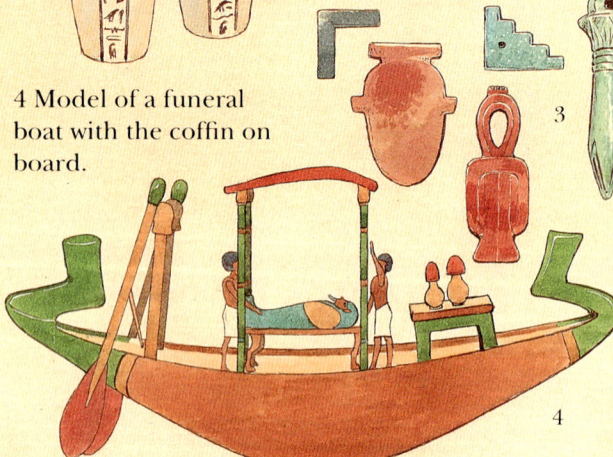

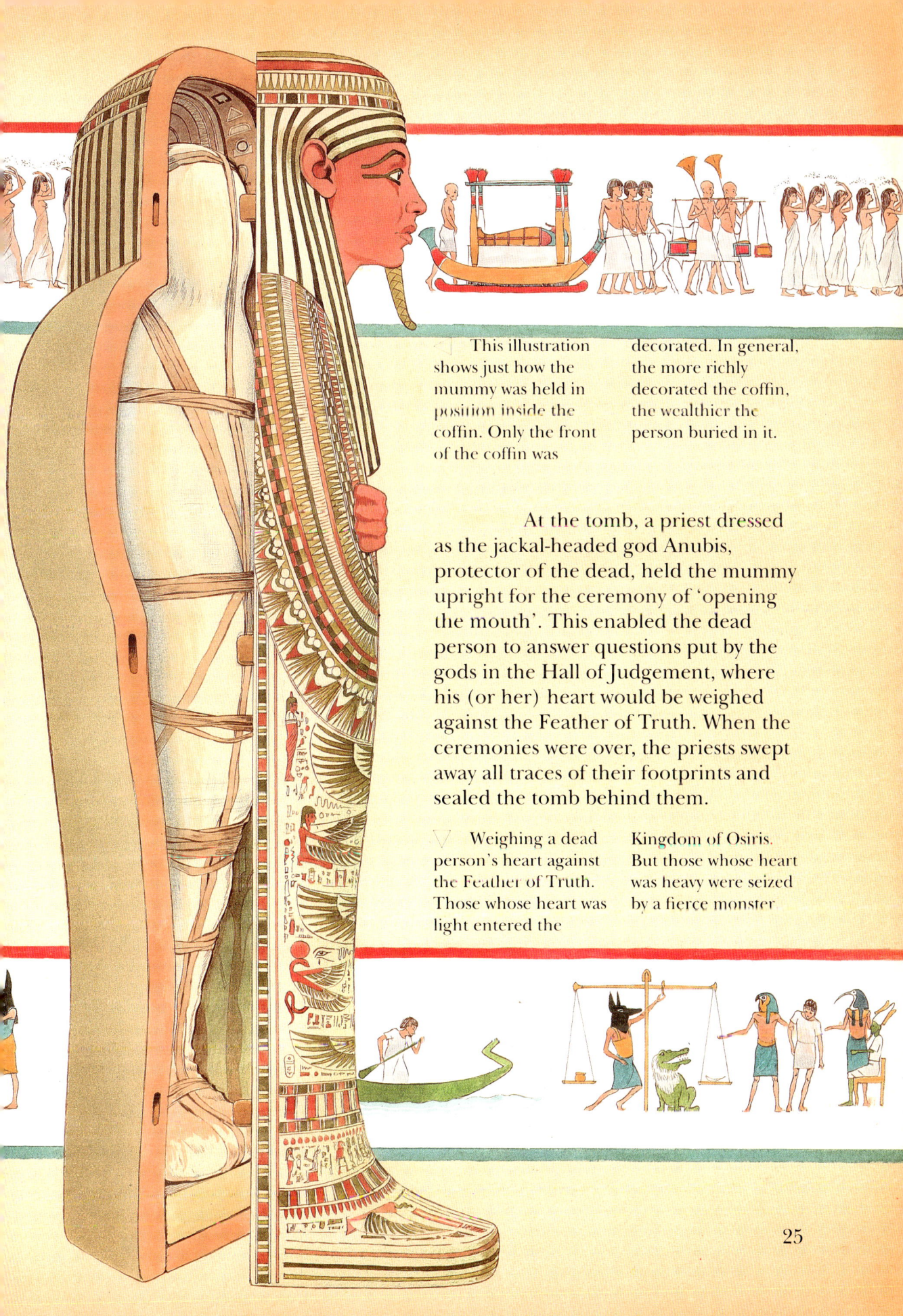

This illustration shows just how the mummy was held in position inside the coffin. Only the front of the coffin was decorated. In general, the more richly decorated the coffin, the wealthier the person buried in it.

At the tomb, a priest dressed as the jackal-headed god Anubis, protector of the dead, held the mummy upright for the ceremony of 'opening the mouth'. This enabled the dead person to answer questions put by the gods in the Hall of Judgement, where his (or her) heart would be weighed against the Feather of Truth. When the ceremonies were over, the priests swept away all traces of their footprints and sealed the tomb behind them.

▽ Weighing a dead person's heart against the Feather of Truth. Those whose heart was light entered the Kingdom of Osiris. But those whose heart was heavy were seized by a fierce monster

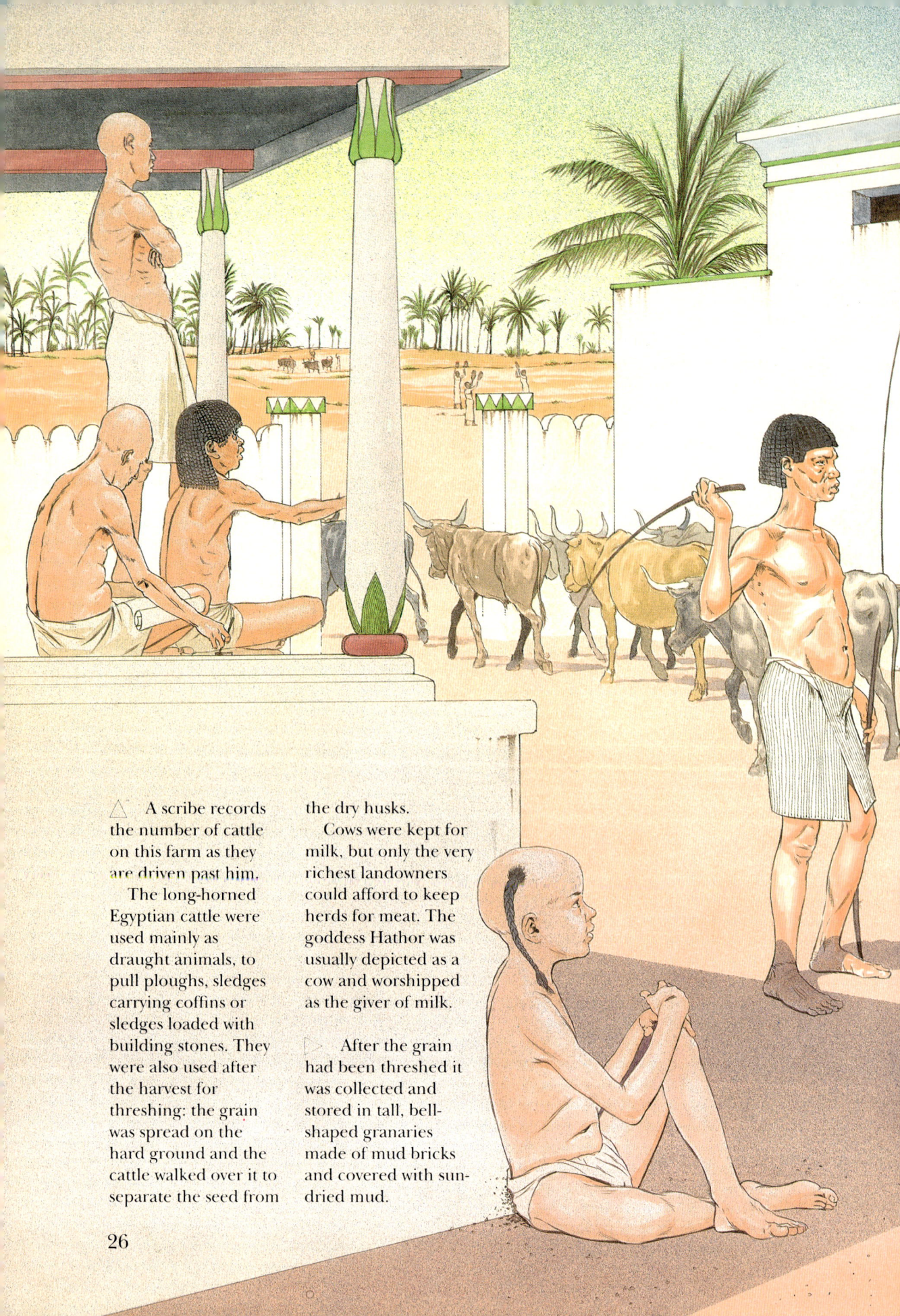

▽ A scribe records the number of cattle on this farm as they are driven past him.

The long-horned Egyptian cattle were used mainly as draught animals, to pull ploughs, sledges carrying coffins or sledges loaded with building stones. They were also used after the harvest for threshing: the grain was spread on the hard ground and the cattle walked over it to separate the seed from the dry husks.

Cows were kept for milk, but only the very richest landowners could afford to keep herds for meat. The goddess Hathor was usually depicted as a cow and worshipped as the giver of milk.

▷ After the grain had been threshed it was collected and stored in tall, bell-shaped granaries made of mud bricks and covered with sun-dried mud.

An Egyptian Farm

MOST PEOPLE WHO LIVED in the country were farmers or worked on the large estates belonging to high officials at the pharaoh's court.

Each year had three seasons: flood, seed-time and harvest. During the flood, when the Nile overflowed, the villages, which were built on higher ground, looked like islands surrounded by the water. There was little farm work to do then. Instead, people fished or made things to sell.

When the floods went down, everyone was busy. There were crops to sow before the sun dried the ground and made it too hard. Then the growing crops had to be watered. Large canals carried water from the Nile to the fields, which were criss-crossed by many smaller water channels.

Everyone had to pay taxes. So, each year after the harvest, the crops were measured. Scribes working for the pharaoh went to all the farms, recording the different crops and working out how much tax had to be paid on each crop. Archaeologists have found many of these tax records.

At the same time, cattle were rounded up, counted and branded with their owner's mark. The number of calves born that year was noted by the scribes. Some might have to be given to the pharaoh as tax.

27

Hunting

TO JUDGE FROM THE many hunting-scenes on the walls of Egyptian tombs, hunting was clearly a very popular pastime. These tomb-paintings show hunting parties setting out for the desert. There, the swift, long-legged hunting dogs would find herds of antelope and gazelle. The hunters, standing in chariots drawn by galloping horses, would spear or shoot the prey with bows and arrows.

Fishing was also popular, and the Nile had many different kinds of fish. They were caught in nets or speared with harpoons. Fishing was enjoyed most by the ordinary people, because it was a way of getting extra food. Any fish not eaten immediately was dried in the sun for future meals.

▽ Harpoons had sharp stone or metal tips on the end of a long wooden handle or shaft. Often a rope was attached to the end of the shaft so that if the wounded animal ran or swam away, the hunter could keep hold of it until other members of the hunting party caught up and closed in for the kill.

▽ Bundles of papyrus reeds bound together made excellent small boats, ideal for fishing or for travelling from village to village along the Nile, but they were no match for an angry hippo. The boats were guided through the reed beds with long poles or the dried stems of particularly strong reeds.

The desert and the river were not the only places to go hunting. In many parts the Nile's banks were marshy and had thick reed beds. These were the home of water birds and, best of all, of the hippopotamus. Hippos could do an enormous amount of damage to crops, trampling into the ground whatever they didn't eat. These huge animals could also be very dangerous. They were hunted from small boats that were really only bundles of papyrus reeds tied together. It didn't take much for an angry, wounded hippo to overturn such a frail craft. Anyone on the boat would fall into the water, and there more danger lurked, for the Nile was full of crocodiles.

Entertaining Friends

GIVING A DINNER PARTY for friends was a very popular form of entertainment among wealthy Egyptian families. Preparing the food often took the cooks all day, before the

guests arrived for the meal in the cool of the evening. Most of the cooking was done over an open fire out of doors, to reduce the risk of fire. Wood was scarce, so reeds from the river were used as a fuel instead.

The meal was usually served under a covered area on the flat roof of the house, which you can see in the illustration on page 4. As the guests arrived, servants gave each one a sweet-smelling lotus flower and put cones of refreshing wax on their heads. The guests of honour and the host and hostess sat on low chairs. Everyone else sat on mats on the floor.

Low tables beside the guests were piled with fruit, vegetables, pastries and a special delicacy: cakes made of date flour sweetened with honey. More servants brought in the main dishes: goose, duck and veal.

While everyone talked and ate, musicians played in the background. Flutes and a kind of lute were popular.

Important Dates

The Ancient Egyptians used a very different system of dating to ours. They calculated the years of each pharaoh separately, beginning again with each new pharaoh. So it is almost impossible to give a precise date for any event in Ancient Egyptian history.

2780 BC	Beginning of the Old Kingdom and the start of Ancient Egypt's greatness. Building of pyramids.
2280	Old Kingdom ends and civil war begins.
2052	Start of the Middle Kingdom and a powerful Egyptian develops.
1778	Middle Kingdom collapses and more unrest and civil war.
1600	The Hyksos gradually take over Egypt.
1567	Beginning of the New Kingdom and a more settled period in Ancient Egypt's history.
1370	Building of Tel-el-Amarna begins.
1290	Rameses II comes to power.
1260	Work begins on the great temple at Abu Simbel.
1223	Death of Rameses II.
1085	End of New Kingdom and decline in Egypt's power and influence.
30	Egypt becomes part of the Roman Empire.

Index

A
Abu Simbel 3, 16–17
Akhenaten 6
amulets 22, 24
Amun 15, 18
Anubis 18, 20, 24, 25
Apis 18
archaeologists 6, 7, 11, 12, 24, 27, 28
army 14–15
Atun 20

B
boats 8, 9, 16, 24, 29
Bubastis 18

C
canopic jars 22, 24
chariots 14, 15, 28
climate 4, 5, 11, 13, 22, 26
clothes 3, 4, 7, 13
crops 8, 27, 28

D
desert 8, 28, 29

F
farming 12, 16–27
Feather of Truth 25

food 4, 6, 26, 30
funerals 24–25
furniture 3, 6, 7, 24, 31

G
Geb 20
gods 10, 17, 18, 20–21

H
Hathor 21, 26
hieroglyphs 16, 17, 21
horses 14, 15, 28
Horus 10, 18, 20
houses 4–5, 6–7
hunting 28–29
Hyksos 15

I
Isis 20

J
jewellery 7, 22

L
life after death 3, 22, 24–25
lotus 5, 31

M
Mediterranean 3, 8

Memphis 18
Middle Kingdom 3
mummies/mummification 22–23, 24–25
musicians 18, 31

N
New Kingdom 3
Nile 3, 5, 6, 8–9, 11, 13, 15, 17, 18, 21, 22, 24, 26, 28, 29, 31
Nubia 3, 9
Nut 18, 20, 21

O
Old Kingdom 3
Osiris 20, 25

P
paper 13
papyrus 7, 13, 29
pharaohs 3, 9, 10–11, 14, 15, 27
Phtah 15
priests 13, 18, 20, 24, 25

R
Rameses II 3, 4, 6, 10, 11, 12, 15, 16, 17, 20, 21
Re 10, 15, 17, 18, 20, 21, 24
religion see gods, pharaohs and temples
Roman Empire 3

S
scarab 20, 24
schools 12–13, 20
scribes 12, 16, 21, 26, 27
servants 4, 24, 31
Seth 15
Shu 20
slaves 17

T
taxes 9, 12, 27
Tel-el-Amarna 6, 8
temples 12, 13, 16–17, 20–21
trade 9, 12

V
vizier 10, 12

W
wigs 4, 13